MW01074950

#LEADERSHIPISAVERB
A 21 DAY CHALLENGE:
Becoming a More Powerful, Effective, and Balanced Student Leader

CHRISCSPEAKS.COM

#LEADERSHIPISAVERB
A 21 Day Challenge:
Becoming a More Powerful, Effective, and Balanced Student Leader

By
Christopher Collins
Foreword by Jarvis Clark

CHRISCSPEAKS.COM

Special discounts are available on quantity purchases by corporations, associations, educators, and others. For details, contact the info@chriscspeaks.com.

Copyright © 2016 by ChrisCSpeaks.com
All rights reserved. No part of this book may be reproduced, scanned, or distributed in any printed or electronic form without permission.
First Edition: November 2016
Printed in the United States of America
ChrisCSpeaks.com

DEDICATION

This Book is dedicated to my wife Samantha, and my three wonderful children Chandler, Laci, and Carson cause y'all love me without my teeth!!
Chase and Ramona you all motivate me to speak the inconvenient truth!
Johnny Quick, the coolest man I know and my grandfather.
Jesus – both God and man 200%

CONTENTS

WHS Class of 2024,

Go forth in confidence to discover what gives your life meaning, your vocation.

¡Adelante!

On My Pathway Conference
Calvin University
April 14, 2022

Steve Beauclair
Program Director

GRCC
GEAR**UP**
Wyoming
grcc.edu/gearup

ACKNOWLEDGEMENT

You said you saw me speaking to large crowds. I always thought that meant I was going to be a rapper. Who would've thought this kid from the south side of Chicago would turn out to have a prophet for a mom!! You called it! You continue to be an inspiration and influence on my thoughts and concepts about leadership. There are folks that have higher titles and more degrees but I would be hard pressed to find someone that has done more for the people they lead than you have. You continue to pour into the lives of your team and give them the tools and opportunity to build a career. You are the epitome of helping people make an impact to the best of their ability. This book is for you and your never wavering support. Your #Leadershipisaverb

I love you Momma

Your Son

FOREWORD

By Jarvis Clark

Are leaders born or made? Upon immediately reading those words, you almost immediately answered the question based on your perspective, which probably stems from your own personal experience. Obviously, because we are able to ask the question and more obviously, because you are able to quickly able to answer, regardless of where you fall, a compelling argument can be made for both sides. People who are tagged with "natural born leader" are usually praised for their charisma, stature, poise in times or extreme stress and seemingly insurmountable obstacles. On the other hand, when you are dependable, reliable, and garner respect from others you are more likely looked upon as a leader; and those are traits that anyone can exude.

As you can see, this question inexplicably has many answers, but doesn't necessarily have any real conclusions. This question over the past couple of years has made me consider maybe we are not asking the right question; or perhaps we are not approaching this paradoxical conundrum with the appropriate perspective. I believe that most people answer this question by immediately thinking about specific people and the awesome and positive feats that they were able to accomplish. Think about it: Jesus Christ, Dr. Martin Luther King Jr., Mahatma Gandhi, Beyoncé (okay maybe not Beyoncé, but you have to admit it was pretty funny reading her name amidst the other three) all did amazing things and because most people admire and respect their accomplishments; When you consider the amount of duress they endured to serve their purpose, their "leader" designation is rarely questioned. Those individuals were able to inspire, galvanize, and move people to achieve purposes bigger than themselves and as a result, we bestow upon them the mantle of extreme leadership often attributing the depth of their feats to a natural phenomenon that most people will never be able to reach, quantify, or even describe.

However, when we examine the likes of Adolph Hitler, the last thing we want to ascribe to him is the title of leader. Most are violently opposed to his actions and his belief system and because of that, we disregard his ability to inspire, galvanize and move people to achieve purposes bigger than themselves. He couldn't be a leader, because he's a bad guy. So if we strip away the accomplishments, and accept that the individuals listed above were able to hold the heart of the people, then why do we discriminate against who is and who is not a leader. Furthermore, if it is all natural, then can we find the genetic code that would assist us in being able to identify who the leaders are so that we can nurture them into being the kind of leader that uses their influence for right and not wrong?

As a higher education administrator, I have seen many students become so enamored with the idea of being a leader, that once they receive the title they behave as though they have arrived. They stop displaying the type of character traits that would confidently lead you to believe that they were good leaders in the first place. Leadership is not about the title you hold, nor is it based on the natural strengths that reside in your personality. However, it is also not true that just because you are great at problem solving, follow the rules, or show any insane amount of organizational and public speaking aptitude, that the mantle of leadership should rest on your head either. Leaders are not born or made. Leaders are those who have learned, indicating that at one point they have had to and still do, to follow others, leverage their natural gifts as tools to execute in various situations, and more importantly live a life where consistency in behavior becomes a guiding principle and not a collection of well-timed fleeting moments.

Christopher R. Collins has always been this type of leader. He has a unique set of natural abilities that allow him to be completely relatable and also push him to achieve higher and accomplish goals bigger than himself. He has leveraged these gifts in such a way that has caused others around him to be inspired, galvanized, and ready to achieve purposes bigger than themselves. His intentionality in teaching people that "Leadership Is a Verb" captures the essence of consistent actions leading to consistent behaviors ultimately resulting in consistent success. He has studied other great leaders, known and unknown, from all walks of life and has benefited from their teachings both directly and indirectly. His practical communication style mixed with his desire to see others be the greatest version of themselves, is just as infectious as it is genuine. He has and continues to be an inspiration to me, I know that after reading this book he will be a great inspiration to you and I am honored and privileged to call him a friend and brother.

#LEADERSHIPISAVERB will be a great foundational tool that will aide you as student leaders to continue to develop the necessary disciplines and philosophies that will transform your worlds and more importantly the worlds of others around you. Enjoy!

INTRODUCTION

Being a student leader is great! It provides opportunities for personal and professional growth, all while meeting the needs of your campus and your community. However, it does come with its challenges. You have to deal with demanding academic schedules, packed social calendars, and take care of your duties as a student leader. Though there is no archetype of a student leader, there is a common trait that most student leaders share, THEY THINK THEY HAVE UNLIMITED ENERGY & TIME!! That is why I 'm never surprised when I am doing a talk at conference or college and students come up to me after and ask, "How do I make it all count and how do I balance it all?"

Having had that question asked to me so many times, I developed a program, Stay in H.A.R.M.'s Way, for that specific reason; developing powerful, effective, and balanced student leaders. This book is an extension of that. It is a practical guide and a 21 day challenge designed to develop the habits and beliefs of Powerful, Effective, and Balanced Student Leaders. After presenting leadership programs at colleges all across the country and in front of thousands of students and administrators I have enough feedback and success stories to know that the concepts work.

#LEADERSHIPISAVERB is designed to help student leaders on every level. If you are just starting your journey into student leadership, start it with these concepts in mind and watch how dope your work will be. If you are already in a leadership role or as my church folk like to say, a seasoned saint; take this 21 Day Challenge as a way to fine tune, correct, or enhance what you are already doing.

You may even discover a fresh perspective that helps you realize you can and should be doing some things differently. If student leadership has you feeling exhausted and ready to throw in the towel, man do you need this challenge! The next 21 days will help you evaluate how to regroup, refocus, and rebuild.

This is not a catch all, fix all book, heck it's less than 105 pages!!! But it is the beginning of a process. It is a guide to relief for the student overwhelmed by the responsibility of their leadership position. It's a blueprint for the new student leader, so they don't get burned out. And a preview for the student nervous about getting involved on campus, letting them know student leadership is challenging but well worth it!

When I was developing this project, I was sure to reach out to various sources to vet my information. Even though I had a great time as a student leader in high school and college, I wanted to make sure the information was relevant, practical, and most importantly, that it WORKED!! So these concepts or principals have been vetted by teachers, counselors, principals, faculty and staff in Student Affairs, ResLife, and Greek Life. Then it was vetted by students! Students that have taken the challenge or heard me discuss the concepts in my talks swear by it.

This challenge attacks student leadership from both sides of the coin. It's very popular for speakers and experts to tell you to find your "why" and the "how" will work itself out...maybe. But I am a process guy. I like to hit you with solutions that you can use and customize for your situation. I will give you tools to discover your "why" and then provide strategies to empower you on "how" to use your new found passion. Most of all, I want to encourage you. I want you to know that no matter where you are in your leadership journey, leadership is always an action word. You are so close to tapping into your potential and doing the great things that you, your campus, and your community needs.

My challenge is to get you to self-discover and then go tackle the needs of your community. I need you to remember a few things as you embark on this 21 Day Challenge:

1. This is not a destination, it's a journey. It's a moving target that depends on your perspective, your experience, and your ability. Don't judge your impact by someone else's success or journey. You may be reading their entire book and comparing it to just a few of your chapters! You know you are in your sweet spot when you feel good about your actions and can support that feeling with your results. That can mean increased attendance at events, more order in meetings, better grades, less stress, etc. You will know when you are "There". So the goal is not to get to THERE but to be THERE more often than not.

2. #Leadershipisaverb Reading this book is pointless if you don't do something!! You are what you do, so get busy!

Be sure to share your thoughts and success with me at

@CHRISCSPEAKS ON

FACEBOOK, TWITTER,

INSTAGRAM, & SNAPCHAT

WHAT IS #LEADERSHIPISAVERB

Before we get started I'm going to give you a cheat sheet. Everything you do for the next 21 days is a set up! It is a set up to get you close to leading using a #LEADERSHIPISAVERB mindset. In order to do that you must always use the following questions as a filter for your interactions as a student leader.

1. What need am I meeting on my campus?
2. What impact will this have on my community?
3. How does this prepare me for my next step?

Your leadership will grow tremendously if you focus on these questions. I won't spoil it for you, but answering those three questions will solve most of the challenges or opportunities for improvement in your personal leadership and communal leadership. Now let's go!

Day 1
Adopt and Resign

The great motivator and orator Zig Ziglar once said that it is our "attitude that determines our altitude." The first step in realizing #LEADERSHIPISAVERB *is to* adopt and resign. Adopt a grateful attitude and resign from laziness. The best leaders work just as hard as, if not harder, than everyone else in their group. How can we reach our goals if we are constantly negative/ungrateful and lazy? We must WORK to reach our potential! So today, stop grumbling, be grateful and work hard, work smarter, and most importantly...work RIGHT!

Why do so many people talk about improving, enhancing, or changing your attitude? Because your thoughts and attitude towards your pursuits have a tremendous impact on your results. And, if we are honest, some of our attitudes could use a tune up. Sometimes we can be our biggest hater. As great as our vision may be, it is in our nature to not only think critically but also be critical of the vision.

To fully realize your potential as a student leader adopt a grateful attitude. I say adopt because it requires you to take something by choice into a relationship. Adoption can be a tough because it requires you make something foreign intimately familiar. Adopting a child, pet, heck even a highway takes some effort and commitment on your part. Adopting signifies an intentional endeavor to get happy with yourself. Part of being an impactful leader is choosing to define your attitude, if not others will do it for you.

I understand you're human and have bad days, but a grateful attitude can help make those days suck less!

As a student leader you have so much to be grateful for (I know I sound like your parents right now, but work with me!): school (if you're in college it's only 16hrs a week), parties every other day – not saying you party every other day but you got options, athletics, clubs, Greek life, reality TV watch clubs, it's the sweetest gig you've likely had so far. Now don't get too caught up in the sweet life! Even with the best attitude, we still have to put in work to reach our potential! Adopting a Grateful attitude will help your aptitude adapt to most situations. After your adoption, you have to resign.

The next part is about resigning from laziness. With all of our modern technology, it has become easier to be more efficient and streamlined in our day to day work. If we're honest, we would admit that most of us are mad lazy!! Not in all aspects of our lives and not all in the same way, but we all fight the battle of laziness. Most of us never realize it because we've been doing it for so long. We tend to rely on our strengths and coast on our natural ability. The best leaders understand that in order to be truly great leaders they must not simply rest on natural abilities but hone them into tools to accomplish their goals. So quit resting on your charisma or your organization's legacy to get you by and invest in your talents so you can excel. It takes some work, but #leadershipisaverb. Resigning from Laziness means you commit to a process of continual refinement and development. Being a dope student leader means making a commitment to always striving to do better.

With Facebook, Twitter, Snapchat, Hulu, Netflix, DVR, and other modern marvels, we sometimes forget what it means to do certain things. I can't remember the last time I looked up something without using Google or Wikipedia. Technology has made things more efficient and readily available. This can lead to a microwave mentality where we expect things to just happen. Not so fast my friend!

Technology makes publicity more streamlined, but nothing beats good old fashioned beating the street with flyers or going out in the community for a little shaking hands and kissing babies. There has to be a balance. We have such great intentions and expectations and we don't understand why after posting the vision for where we want to take our organization on the Facebook page and tweeting it, the entire campus doesn't get fired up and fall strategically into place bum-rushing our events and knocking down the door to join. Maybe people are just not into the bottle cap collection club you started! Or maybe they don't know you're collecting them for a charity to donate money for students on your campus affected by cancer. Being a more powerful, effective, and balanced leader ain't easy; it requires elbow grease and clear communication. We can't rely solely on our vision and intentions to lead for us. We have to inject our powerful vision with work ethic and effectively convey our intentions with passion, to inspire others to work along with us so we can have a balanced life and not do it all ourselves.

Just the other day I was complaining about how long it took a webpage to load on my phone. Really!? I was watching a movie with my kids and they asked,

"Why is someone talking on a black brick? And is that a lunch box with a shoulder strap?" They were talking about an original cell phone!! It was at that very moment I realized complaining about how long it takes a webpage to load on my phone, was ridiculous! I should be celebrating and grateful that I have a super computer in my pocket. As student leaders we sometimes get caught up in the same trap. We ask "Why can't we submit proposals online?", "Why is tweeting the meeting time not enough to get a good turnout?", or my favorite… "I texted you to do it!!" I'm not bashing technology but networking and socializing are still best done in person. Leadership is still best done face to face, building one relationship at a time. It takes effort, dedication, and more importantly passion! Your organization will not be great just because you say it is. You have to efficiently guide your org into a position of influence/power through strategic programming, thoughtful community service, and providing solutions to meet the needs of the students on your campus. Leadership is work, it doesn't matter if you're a student, administrator, or CEO. So today, adopt a grateful attitude, work hard, work smarter, and most importantly…work RIGHT! It'll be your first step in your journey to powerful student leadership and operating in #LEADERSHIPISAVERB.

- What can you do today to adopt a more positive attitude? What can you say or do?

- What bad habit or area of laziness do you need to resign from?

- What practical things can you do to get and maintain a spirit of gratefulness?

ADOPTING
A GRATEFUL ATTITUDE

WILL HELP YOUR APTITUDE ADAPT
TO MOST SITUATIONS.

Day 2
Potential is the World's Greatest Dichotomy

Potential; one of the most dangerous words in the English language. It is also referred to as upside, raw talent, and being unpolished. But no matter how you shape it, it's still dangerous. Just ask Michael Jordan about potential. Potential is why he drafted Kwame Brown straight out of high school with the number one pick in the NBA draft (FYI that was a bad idea Mike). Kwame had all of the tools to be a dominant NBA player; height, speed, footwork, etc. Kwame eventually became a decent player. He actually stuck around the league for about 11 years and made over 60 million dollars in earnings. That's a long and profitable career. But Kwame Brown will go down as one of the biggest bust in NBA Draft history all because of one word, potential. He wasn't drafted to be decent or serviceable. He was drafted to be a franchise player, a corner stone that his team could build on for years to come. He just never quite got made it. You might be able to relate to Kwame. You might have all the tools to be a great student leader. You might have even been drafted/elected to be the organization superstar and help your org run the campus for the next few years. But potential alone is not enough.

Potential is why numerous students and employees are given projects that stretch their capabilities, hoping to tap into some seldom used power or insight. But potential is also the reason why folks make excuses for a less than stellar performance.

So often I hear teachers, professors, and parents talk about potential. "If they just get their head outta their butt they would see they have so much potential!" And here lies the issue with this powerful word, it's conditional and normally accompanied by "if". And as my grandma used to tell me, "If a bullfrog had wings it wouldn't bump its behind." Potential is so dangerous because it is trapped in a place deep within our spirit that only we have the key to unlock, but unfortunately for us and the world waiting on us to unlock it; we rarely see our own potential. And when you don't recognize or acknowledge your greatness you also don't recognize or acknowledge your responsibility to live up to and realize that greatness. We are all born with the potential to make progressive and noticeable differences in the lives of our families and communities. Whether we recognize that calling is up to us.

But how do we recognize something that we can't see or feel but people around us are always referencing? How can we finally meet this specter that's been following some of us around since childhood? First, you have to accept that you are connected to something greater than yourself and that human beings have a purpose beyond personal gain (notice I said beyond, not in lieu of). Being successful in your personal endeavors is an important step in gaining the confidence required to fully live up to your potential.

Second, you have to fight to find your passion and purpose like a water buffalo trying to escape the clutches of a crocodile!!

I know that's a little dramatic, but that's just the type of fight you need to have in your efforts to find your passion and purpose. Finding your passion and purpose takes some people years of soul searching and others are born with it tattooed on their forehead. Most of us fall in the middle and just need a little intentional effort and thought. Intentional effort to connect to activities and causes that inspire you and challenge you to do and be better. Intentional thoughts of positive affirmation and motivation that provide you a reminder of how dope you are and how valuable you are to your community.

Living up to your potential is important because of the negative effects of failing to reach it. On a personal level, never tapping in to your potential means never being fulfilled. It's like being at a buffet in Vegas and only eating salad!! And on a community level, never tapping into your potential means a need or yearning for your community goes unmet, effectively restraining the potential of the community as a whole.

Don't let others be the only one to see your potential. Recognize your power and use it, today!

- **What are some things/strengths that others see in you that you don't see in yourself?**

- **What are some areas you are naturally talented in? How can those talents benefit you, your campus, and your community?**

WE ARE ALL BORN WITH THE POTENTIAL TO MAKE PROGRESSIVE AND NOTICEABLE DIFFERENCES IN THE LIVES OF OUR FAMILIES AND COMMUNITIES. WHETHER WE RECOGNIZE THAT CALLING IS UP TO US.

Day 3
<u>You was who you was</u>
<u>before you got here</u>

I remember when I heard Jay-Z rap, "you can try to change but that's just the top layer, you was who you was before you got here" and paid it no attention because I was too busy rocking to the song. But as I was talking to my grandfather about leaving corporate America to pursue my dream of being a speaker, I sort of heard the line again when my grandmother said,

"you are who you are son and can't nobody stop you from dreaming. Even when your dreams is crushed, they gon' always whisper to you every now and then. Cause that's how God made you!" I immediately began thinking about the power in the two phrases. No matter the circumstances or challenges, we are who we are when we get here, anything outside of our natural inclination is a superficial change. Now before you get depressed because you weren't born with a silver spoon, dashing good looks, and athletic ability...I want you to dig deeper.

For the purpose of this book, let's end the debate about what you are or are not born with. We are all born with a destiny of personal GREATNESS; a purpose that maximizes our abilities for the good of our families and communities. The issue is that our environments and more importantly our responses to our environments are increasingly moving us away from the spirit of Greatness that God spoke into our lives to one focused on success. This means we need to be mindful of our environment and how we react to our environment.

As a leader you will quickly find out that there are some situations that are just out of your control. For example, you might not be able to control your roommate, the people on your planning committee, or your overbearing advisor. But none of those things are excuses to not be great. That roommate may make the journey sloppy and stinky, the folks on your committee might make it harder than what it needs to be, and that advisor may test your patience to the very last nerve but none of them should stop you. Because in those moments, you have to focus on the one thing you can always manage and that is your response.

On Day 1 we discussed how your attitude can make or break you. That hasn't changed just because we are few days into this thing. Your resolve and response in the face of the inevitable stress and drama that can accompany student leadership is a reflection of how deeply you believe in your purpose. When the drama comes, it can and will shake your resolve but it shouldn't break you or deter you from reaching your goals. When your environment gets challenging, it's a good idea to change the scenery even if it's just temporary. Take an hour to regroup in the library, grab a bite to eat with some good friends, or do an activity that allows to you refocus; anything that changes the scenery and resets your mind.

In those moments when the environment is negative and there is nothing you can do about it, remember "you was who you was before you got here" and tough times won't change the fact that you are the dopest of the dope, the baddest of the bad, and the freshest of the fresh. You. Can. Not. Be. Faded.

YOU. CAN. NOT.

BE FADED.

Are you listening to the echo of GREATNESS God whispered into your spirit? Depending on our situations some of us may have to listen harder than others but it's there. There is a voice in your spirit to achieve, motivate, inspire, and dream! Listen to that voice. It is essential in your development as a person and teaches you how to lead by the experiences you gain following your dreams. Before we were conceived God spoke GREATNESS & PURPOSE into our lives. The things that have and will happen in our lives have shaped us for the message of GREATNESS God spoke into our existence. Today listen to the echoes of the words God spoke.

* **How do you plan to escape/get away when your environment is negative?**

* **How would your campus look if it were perfect? How can you and your organization help move the campus towards that vision?**

* **What are some ways you can demonstrate your personal greatness?**

Day 4
You DOn't Grind
You don't Shine

Seriously, Mike Jones (who? Mike Jones! just google him, lol) was on to something here. How can you expect to shine if you aren't willing to grind!?! Being a more powerful leader means you must work at perfecting your craft, even those that come naturally to us. It is this continuous honing, or "grinding" out of imperfections, of our skills that prepares us for our moments in the spotlight, our SHINE. Malcolm Gladwell, in his book "Outliers", proposed the 10,000 hour theory that basically stated 10,000 hours of "deliberate practice" is the baseline to become world class at something. 10,000 hours plus some talent is just enough time to grind out the rough edges and become really good at something. I'm not sure 10,000 hours of practice would make me a world class singer, but I would be missing the talent portion of the equation. Interestingly enough, Malcolm Gladwell and Mike Jones were sort of saying the same thing and when you apply the theory to how you lead, it helps get you understand #LEADERSHIPISAVERB.

Your org can only rest on or blame its laurels and history for so long. Eventually, you have to do your part to build on the successful track record or rebuild after less than stellar results. Being a great student leader is not easy, but it's worth it if you work it (shout out to Missy Elliiot)! When you first get a knife, its cuts like a..... like a hot knife through butter. But over time the blade begins to dull and to get the knife back to peak performance, you have to grind it out! Being a leader is no different.

BEING A GREAT STUDENT LEADER

IS NOT EASY, BUT ITS WORTH IT IF YOU WORK IT!

When you are holding meetings, putting on events, and still being an excellent student, it can wear on you. But keep grinding! Keep working! Don't be afraid of the process that leads to excellence. Most people don't get to where they want to be not because they lack ability, but because they lack grit; the willingness to consistently dedicate time and effort toward a goal

Here is a funny thing about the grind, it's not easy but it's popular. If you let social media tell it, everyone is on their grind. Everyone is making major moves or killing the game. In reality, IF everyone was truly on their grind, our campuses would look and feel differently than they currently do. Our orgs would not constantly struggle with apathy and turnover. You might hear a lot of folks talking about being on their "grind" or how they "stay on the grind" but we both know they ain't really bout that life! I'm just kidding; you should be so focused on your grind and work that you are too busy to pay attention to other folks.

Both the grind and the shine look different for every leader, so don't compare your journey to someone else's. Your grind may be learning Robert's Rules of Order or learning how to write effective proposals. My grind was learning how to effectively delegate. I had to intentionally put myself in situations where delegating was the only way for an event or activity to be successful. It was hard! I hated letting go and not being in control and sometimes I thought asking people to help meant I was being lazy or weak.

Thankfully I had great people around me that I was able to be transparent with and that I trusted to hold me accountable to be the best leader I could be. They helped me to shift my mindset and realize that sharing the load wasn't a sign of weakness, but instead a show of confidence in the team and their abilities. Together we helped each other do some great things on our campus and became wonderful friends in the process. Our shine was always different too. Some of us liked the limelight and the attention while others were satisfied with knowing they played a critical role in the success and of an org. Either way, we made both the grind and the shine of student leadership a critical part of our journey to living #LEADERSHIPISAVERB.

- **What is something you need to work harder at or improve upon? (Being more organized, on time, better study habits, etc.) How do you plan on getting better?**

- **How do you prefer to shine/be recognized? In public? In private? With a group? Individually? Why do you prefer it that way?**

- **What is your recognition love language? (How do you want to be rewarded when you succeed? Gifts, props on social media, internal recognition, etc.?**

- **Be sure to share how you like to be recognized and rewarded with the folks in a position to do so.**

Day 5
Find Your Passion, Find Your Greatness

Identify the things you are passionate about and discover ways to integrate them into your life and your organization roles. This way you begin to learn about things you love and in turn you can LIVE WHAT YOU LEARN. "Passion Distinguishes the Difference between Success and Greatness.....Where does your Passion Lie?" This leadership thing can be challenging (I promise it's not all bad, I just refuse to over promise and under deliver) so you need to have something that motivates you to keep pushing. In my Stay in H.A.R.M.'s Way presentation, I tell students that there are an infinite amount of opportunities to get involved on campus but you only have a finite amount of time to give. The best leaders understand that they can't run every group on the yard. If you can hold 9 offices, sit on 6 committees, and volunteer for 11 different charities and maintain a social life and academic excellence you are a super hero and this principle doesn't apply to you!! But if you weren't born on krypton, you may want to be selective about the activities in which you engage.

...THERE ARE AN

INFINITE AMOUNT

OF OPPORTUNITIES

TO GET INVOLVED ON CAMPUS BUT

YOU ONLY HAVE

A FINITE AMOUNT

OF TIME TO GIVE

Ask yourself, "Self, what are we really good at?" Think about the things that come naturally to you and figure out a way to integrate them into the things you care about. For example, if you really like to write then maybe you can manage the blog or press releases for your org. If you enjoy doing community service, being the community service chair may seem like an obvious choice, unless you don't really like people. Then you may just want to be in charge of finding the community service project and let someone that likes people do the rest. In all seriousness, we perform better when we are passionate about our performance. I can't tell you what event had me staying up late writing proposals with my boys back in college, but I can tell you that those moments were worth it because we believed in what we were doing. Let your passion fuel your greatness.

The best leaders, and this is true on a campus or in a corporation, do their best work when they are invested. What better way to be invested in your org or event than to believe in what you are doing? Not only does it make leadership more enjoyable but it also makes it more rewarding. There are some people that would probably be successful at anything they did, they are just that driven or competitive. But they are only GREAT at the things they were meant to do. I know finding your passion sounds like some metaphysical journey filled with incense and meditation, but it's not necessarily that deep. By now you will have likely been involved in a few group projects and maybe one or two organizations or groups. Maybe your involvement was from church, sports teams, or youth clubs, but it's still relevant. Think back to your level of engagement in those activities. What did you enjoy? What did you dislike? Was there an assignment, cause, or activity that motivated you to practice or work harder towards a goal?

These are the type of simple questions that can help you find your passion. Moreover, the great thing about your passion is that it can change and isn't singular. You can be passionate about different things at different times of your collegiate career and with varying levels. When I was freshman all I wanted to do was put on the biggest event in campus history! I was passionate about being recognized and affirmed by my peers and the university.

As I got more involved on campus and my interest became more nuanced I really started to be more specific about the work I did on campus and the results I wanted to see. I wasn't worried about the size of the event anymore, I was concerned with the impact and the legacy the event created. When it was all said and done, I was able to look back and be proud of the work I was a part of and realize that I lived #LEADERSHIPISAVERB.

- **What are you passionate about? How does that passion connect with your purpose and your plan?**

- **What are some some things you are naturally good at?**

- **How has your focus/passion changed, grown, or developed since you started your student leadership journey?**

Day 6
Be Account-Able!:
Do you and Do it Well

Being accountable means taking stock or census of your abilities and your areas of growth and adjusting accordingly. This means you have to be somewhat self-aware and do an honest self-assessment. If you haven't already, a good start for this self-assessment is anyone of the leadership models that tells you your letters or color. Are you a blue green or an orange yellow? Are you INTJ or EFNP? If you are still lost, I'm talking about the True Colors or Myers-Briggs assessments that are popular on campuses and in corporations. You will undoubtedly participate in one of these great assessments, but whatever you do don't live by the results. Your leadership can't be defined by a set of colors or letters matched to a personality trait. Your #leadershipisaverb and will be defined by your impact on campus. If you have been in a formal leadership role before, you can look at that experience and determine what you did well and what you need to improve. You just have to be honest with yourself.

If you were always late to the meeting, even when you told yourself the meeting started at 7:30 just so you could show up at 8, you might want to take a look at that. That was me, smh. I was "that" guy. Great vision, good ideas, but start without him, he will not be on time. In order to grow and develop, I had to take a personal assessment. At first glance I thought my issue was punctuality.

With some deeper thought and input from people I trusted, I realized it wasn't necessarily a punctuality issue but an issue with over commitment. I had a hard time saying no and a horrible sense of how long things actually took! What helped me tremendously was setting a quota on how many projects or orgs I would participate in and intentionally spacing my meetings at least 45 mins apart whenever possible. This allowed me to be my engaged sometimes longwinded self a little easier. I also set the expectation for the meeting in the very beginning by saying things like, "I have another meeting at 7, so we have to be wrapped up by 6:15, 6:30 at the latest." This allowed everyone to be on the same page.

I was a charismatic leader and that allowed me to be persuasive and get buy in from the group. But my growth happened when I held myself accountable to make sure my character matched my charisma and that my leadership was based on content not just flash. The most interesting thing about me holding myself accountable was the response of the people I worked with and for. Whether we admit it or not, taking on a formal leadership role means volunteering to be watched and scrutinized. Once I began to consistently take account for my abilities I became a better leader and a better member. When I began to set and live up to a personal standard of excellence, it began to pour over into a culture of excellence in the orgs I worked in.

Great leaders are accountable for themselves as well as those around them. One of the biggest issues in organizational or group dynamics is accountability.

That dynamic is evident even more so in student organizations because in large part, the activities rely on volunteers. Most of us can relate to someone dropping the ball on an assignment that they volunteered to do! I mean you don't have to lie to kick it Craig.

If you knew you didn't have time to do it, you shouldn't have volunteered! But most of the time the ball is not dropped out of malice. Folks don't want to fail, but just like I had a problem saying no to helping out in various orgs, some people have a hard time admitting a task is beyond their scope of time, ability, or desire.

Students are busy and if they haven't mastered how to identify and overcome time killers, time slips away all too often and the things they truly prioritize take precedent and that's not likely to be an organization or a committee report. When you take on or assign a task that is totally outside of someone's wheelhouse you are not taking account for their abilities and might be projecting your skills on to them! Most folks will try to do a task, even if it's out of their skill set or reach but without the proper support even the best intentions fall short of expectations. And the worst possible thing to do as a leader is to put someone in a position or role they really don't want to or aren't equipped to accept. We must put people in a position to succeed. They might take one for the team, as long as it doesn't require any true commitment or grit. As soon as the task becomes a challenge it will go to the back of the priority list. Why? "Cause they didn't want to do that mess in the first place!"

make sure my character matched my charisma and my leadership WAS BASED ON CONTENT NOT JUST FLASH

To stop this foolishness we must first address the culture of our orgs and then we have to change the way we build teams. To address the culture, we have to understand there are two types of leadership, authoritative or collaborative. Authoritative leadership creates a culture where ideas and responsibility mostly flow from the top down. If you tend to come up with the idea and then assign folks tasks to make your vision a reality...you might be an authoritative leader.

Collaborative leadership creates a culture where the flow of ideas and responsibility is a two way, multi-lane highway. The vision for an event is formed through a cooperative discussion and the responsibility for its implementation is assigned based off ability and availability. We have to create an inclusive culture where, when at all possible, we lead through collaborative efforts instead of authoritative ones. When everyone has contributed to the culture and feels valued, they are more likely to lend their abilities and talents to fulfilling the vision. We also have to set an expectation of excellence and then provide people the tools to reach that expectation. For that, you have to start building better teams.

Once you have established a culture of collaboration, it is easier for people in your org to see the value they bring to projects and in turn more likely that they will be more engaged in fulfilling their responsibilities to the project. It also helps to assemble teams with the end in mind. When at all possible, put people in a position to succeed by giving responsibilities that align with their skill set or the support to help them develop an area of opportunity.

In other words don't Pookie from New Jack City ya people!! Who thought it was a good idea to put a crack head undercover in a crack house?! Accountability, both personal and organizational, is about believing in the purpose/person. When we see the value of what we do, it's much easier to hold ourselves accountable to do it.

- **Are you a Collaborative Leader or an Authoritative Leader? What are some examples where both can be beneficial? How will you work on strengthening both of these leadership styles?**

- **How can you learn more about your team/org so that you can put people in a position to succeed?**

Day 7
Don't Wait, G.R.O.W.

Whether you are richer or poorer, in the penthouse or the projects, running the yard or getting run off of it, we all want to GROW! As student leaders, we all want bigger and better. We want better programming, more attendance to meetings, and more recognition on campus. In order to do bigger and better we have to grow and redefine our student leadership abilities and become more powerful, effective and balanced student leaders. Your growth will guide you to make your leadership a verb.

It doesn't matter if you are working your way back from financial ruin like Dave Ramsey (Google him, his story is amazing), relinquishing your wealth to help save the world like Bill Gates & Warren Buffet, a student leader trying to capitalize on a great event, or an organization trying to bounce back from a poor year, our sights are set on bigger and better. Regardless of where we stand on the totem pole, growth is difficult, and that is why everyone is not doing bigger and better. However, the strategy for growth is the same for those enjoying the view from the top or facing insurmountable odds from the bottom; you have to G.R.O.W.; expand your horizons and stretch your abilities to fill in the gaps.

Growth usually requires the right set of conditions at the right time, with the proper stimulus. The stimulus is really the key, it is what jump starts the expanding of your horizons and fuels the stretching of your abilities.

YOUR WILL WILL WHEN YOUR DREAMS CAN'T!

I was trying to grow some plants in my garden (actually I was having them planted, but I digress) and I could not figure out why they would not grow. My neighbor on the other hand had a yard that looked like it belonged in Busch Gardens. When I asked him his secret, he told me it was MiracleGro. It was how he was able to have bigger and better flowers than the rest of the block. He mixed it in with his soil to provide the stimulus needed to initiate and sustain the growth of his plants. For those of us seeking to redefine our student leadership and grow into more powerful, effective, and balanced student leaders, we need to find this same stimulus to start and sustain our personal and organizational growth. Here is a formula for your very own MiracleG.R.O.W.

Goals

We have all heard of S.M.A.R.T. goals, but they can only get you so far. Expanding your horizons requires you to reach for the stars. Set a goal that is only attainable if you operate at your most powerful, effective, and balanced capacity, something that is going to make you stretch! Picture yourself the master of your craft, your community a thriving utopia, or any other flowery superlatives you can come up with. Set a goal of greatness. *NO MATTER HOW GRAND – SET BIG GOALS.* Without them you will never know how close you are to your destination. Big goals help create powerful visions.

Reality

After you set your goals, align them with reality. If you want to be a top executive or graduate at the top of your class (which are not as closely related as people make them seem), do some dang research!!

Figure out how the people doing what you want to do did it and pattern (not copy) your plan accordingly. If you want to have the most community service hours on campus (even though you only have 10 members and only 4.6 show up to service events), figure out what your campus counts for community service hours and figure out how your group can maximize the parameters of the system. *REALIZE GREAT GOALS REQUIRE A GREAT DEAL OF WORK!* To maximize your work, be effective; eliminate doing stuff 'just because' and do the things that matter first!

Options

Keep your options open. It is perfectly fine, and incredibly intelligent, to adjust your plan/focus to maximize your current conditions. Some of the greatest comebacks happen after halftime adjustments are made! Don't be too proud or arrogant to believe that your original plan was so gangsta that it was bulletproof!! Situations, "people," and you have one thing in common....they all change! And your goals and plans should leave room to accommodate those changes. Also, educate yourself on the resources that are available to you. Are there any partnerships or special assistance offered by your school or job that can help reach your goals? *ALWAYS HAVE OPTIONS.*

Will

This is the most essential part of the G.R.O.W. strategy. You can set all the goals in the world and have all of your options open and primed, but if you never START the process, it doesn't matter. As a leader, it is your responsibility to inspire and ignite the WILL of your group. It is your WILL that provides the catalyst to achieve your aggressive goals. Your WILL can reshape your reality and create options that you never expected. Your WILL can motivate you to conquer your failures and drive your successes. Your WILL will when your dreams can't! Your WILL puts the Miracle in your G.R.O.W.!!!!

Don't be afraid to step up and take roles that require you to be uncomfortable or challenged. Those are some the most rewarding experiences in leadership. There is a difference between being unqualified or in over your head and inexperienced. When you are in over your head, you don't have the ability to do the task at hand. You just don't have the juice!! But being inexperienced simply means you have yet to maximize your abilities. You have the skills required to do the task, you just may not have done it often. Sometimes my moms would buy us clothes that were just a little too big. We'd be in the dressing room looking at her cuff a pant leg, roll a sleeve, or adjust a waist line. The clothes didn't fit us at the moment, but she would say, "the way y'all grow, it will fit next week!" I don't know if it was really a week but I do know I remember growing out of those clothes more than I remember them being too big. On your journey to become a more powerful student leader, don't be afraid to GROW into a position because now you know how to G.R.O.W.!

Know When Good Enough is Good Enough

Raise your hand if you want to execute a just 'aight event. If you raised your hand, smack it down and do better! No one sets out to be just ok or average and I don't intend to guide you towards that mind set now. #LEADERSHIPISAVERB is not about average leadership, you can do that in your sleep! I do however want to address a trend that I've seen on campuses where orgs will plan a thing to death. I get it, you want your org and subsequently your events to be lit. In order for that to happen you have to plan everything down to the teeth. What's the hashtag going to be? Will there be a special guest? Where will we host the event? These are all valid questions and as I discuss on Day 13, it's critical to know when to sweat the small stuff. It's just as critical to know when good is good enough.

Does there have to be a separate meeting for every decision? Do you really need 6 committees for an ice cream social program at the residence hall? Are you really going to ask the graphic designer for 11th draft of the flyer for the multicultural affairs social just because you want a different font? There is such thing as too much analysis, it's actually called analysis paralysis.

Analysis paralysis or paralysis by analysis is the state of over-analyzing (or over-thinking) a situation so that a decision or action is never taken, in effect paralyzing the outcome. You would think that this would be an issue just for the super organized and over thinkers of the world, but nope it affects most leaders.

As a leader you want the product to be a representation of the labor. You know the hard work and late nights that were spent planning and executing a project and you want the rest of the campus to see that as well. I appreciate that effort and hopefully your campus does too (if not jump to Day 12), however your campus needs your best not your perfection. You have to know when good enough is good enough.

This is easier said than done. We seem to be preparing, and getting our minds right, when we should be doing. We should always strive for perfection, but with the full knowledge that we will never achieve it. It's only so much planning you can do, then it's time to ACT or get off the pot. I subscribe to the Fire, Aim, and Ready philosophy. When you have a great idea or event, plan it and plan it well then make it happen!! This is where the real work begins.

FIRE - EXECUTE
AIM - EVALUATE
READY - EXECUTE BETTER

#LEADERSHIPISAVERB

<u>Fire</u> – Execute the event to the best of your ability. This doesn't make you exempt from planning or preparing for an event, but it does mean that you can't plan stuff to death! Plan for what you can account for and adjust for the rest. Always leave room in your plans for adjustments and growth.

<u>Aim</u> - Now that you have put your event or program out there, you can review the results and adjust. It's tough to get it just right the first time out the box, that's why there are 100 versions of the iPhone! However, you produce a product to meet a need on your campus and then let the campus tell you if you hit the mark. Build-in a way for participants to give feedback on the event/program and determine how you can better execute the program or more closely meet the need. Better yet, determine if the event needs to be repeated at all.

<u>Ready</u> - now that you have experience and data you are ready. You are ready to plan and implement the next idea with the experience of having launched a project before and the data of what your campus wants from your org. With those two arrows in your quiver you'll continue to get closer and closer to the bull's-eye.

Fire with a shotgun focus, it allows you to hit a wider target. **Aim** with a pistol focus, it's more specific but still versatile. Then you are **ready** to zero in with sniper rifle focus and hit the bullseye!! Fire. Aim. Ready. Get stuff done because...#LEADERSHIPISAVERB

Day 9
Find the Win-Win:
The Secret to Running the Yard

How do you define running the yard? Is it having the most attendance at your events? The most events? Having the most members? How do you know that you are running the yard? I know how I defined running the yard....DOMINATION!   I wanted to have the most events, the best events, and most people at the events. I even wanted to be the person in the org responsible for inviting the most people!   I wanted the only orgs that mattered on campus to be the orgs that mattered to me. That wasn't very nice nor was it very successful.   I quickly alienated people in other orgs; heck some of the folks in my org didn't like me. It is impossible for one group to be all things to all people. It's also counterproductive for the growth of the org, its members and the campus as a whole.

When trying to maximize your leadership opportunities it's important to have the proper view of what running the yard means. Always look for the win-win when it comes to running the yard. Focusing on the win-win allows you to lead with the proper perspective. You want your org to win and your campus to win, in order for that to happen other orgs have to succeed as well.   Or at least not fail because of your direct efforts. Healthy competition is good and pushes us to do our best, but domination shouldn't be the goal. The win-win focus is an intentional effort to guide your org to living its vision and mission to the fullest of its capabilities while still supporting and encouraging other orgs to do the same.

You have to be intentional with your interactions with other orgs. Your support of other activities on your campus helps to build better camaraderie and campus synergy. It's critical that we never become so consumed with running the yard that we sabotage other orgs. I don't care how you justify it, it's never ok to be petty! IF you have to speak ill of another org for you org to shine, you have bigger problems on your hand than being a hater. You might be in "that" org.

No one wants to be in "that" org. Don't front, you know the org I'm talking about. Ok, answer this question – When you see this orgs name on a flyer you know there will be like 4 people at the event and 3 of them will be members. Yeah, that org. It's not your responsibility to keep another org up and running but you can do your part to support your fellow students and build the rapport between groups. When a majority of the orgs on campus are living up to their potential, the campus is in a better place.

HEALTHY COMPETITION IS GOOD AND PUSHES US TO DO OUR BEST, BUT DOMINATION SHOULDN'T BE THE GOAL.

3 Ways to have the Win-Win Focus with Other Orgs

1. Plan at least one event with another organization.
   Bonus Points if that org doesn't share your same demographic targets

2. When at all possible plan a meeting to attend another org's event
   Bonus Points if you publicize that event like it's your own

3. Be flexible with your dates and times for events to give members/campus time to support you and other orgs
   Bonus Points if you actually meet before the semester with other e-boards and plan a semester calendar

Day 10
Faith it 'til you make it:
Let your attitude dictate your situation, not the other way around.

Let's face it, we all have bad days. The happiest most fulfilled people in the world still wake up on the wrong side of the bed, it happens. It is natural for people to be in a funk or a sour mood from time to time. Sometimes things simply don't go as we planned and we are disappointed. On those bad days, it can be tough to want to get out of bed, don't even think about going to a meeting or event. But as a leader sometimes you don't have a choice. You have to be at the board meeting or you are the MC for an event. There are times when our attendance is mandatory and our moods don't want to cooperate.

I always think about this book my daughter was reading, "Alexander and the Terrible, Horrible, No Good, Very Bad Day" by Judith Viorst. If you haven't read this book, you should. Yes. I. Am. Serious. In this children's book, Alexander has the worst day in the history of little kids. Nothing goes right for my man Alex. He wakes up with gum in his hair, has beef with his best friends, and then has to eat lima beans for dinner! Man hold up! In the book, Alex is always trying to move to Australia to get away from his emotions, but eventually he buckles down and deals with his issues. I know sometimes we feel like running away when we have bad days or are in a bad mood, but that won't always change the situation.

We have to face the source of an issue to conquer it and that's not a quick fix so in the meantime; Faith it til you make it. I'm not suggesting you fake a certain type of personality to appease others, I'm suggesting you speak your reality into existence. Some of you may have just checked the cover of the book and asked, "How is this practical?" I know that positive affirmation gets a lot of flak and comes off hokey or pseudoscience. However there is practical truth to speaking life to your situation. You may have heard the phrase "Attitude reflects Leadership" but attitude also EFFECTS leadership. If you were to take poll on the most important characteristics of a leader, attitude would be one of the top attributes. Because frankly, no one wants to work with someone that has a stank attitude!

Your ability to be transparent with your emotions but still show the ability to not let them control your outlook is a powerful way to cement the character of your leadership. I'm not asking you to pretend that you're not having a bad day, I'm asking you to acknowledge it and fight through it all in the same breath. A bad day doesn't excuse us from our responsibilities nor is it an excuse to be a jerk. Even on your worse days, speak positive affirmations of faith into your situation and watch how quickly that becomes a part of the culture of your organization. When you have a group of folks that won't let a bad day stop them from believing in the mission watch how often your org reaches its goals.

A BAD DAY DOESN'T
EXCUSE US
FROM OUR
RESPONSIBILITIES
NOR
IS IT AN EXCUSE
TO BE A JERK

Day 11
Be YOU:
Because Being Fake is too Hard

I remember my first time being exposed to a fraternity; it was in my grandmother's kitchen when is like nine! My cousin Pooh was dating a Que and telling me about the stereotypes of the different Black Greek-lettered organizations. The Que's were wild and crazy, the Sigmas were country, the Iotas were nerdy, the Kappas were players and the Alpha's were too serious to have fun. I was enthralled by her stories about parties and pledging and stepping. At the time the community service stuff didn't appeal to me, I'm just being honest. She told me a story about how someone at a party was asking her about her boyfriend and called him Omega Kenneth. I was so confused I asked, "I thought his name was Kenneth, does pledging change your name too?" She laughed and said no but it changes how folks view you. It typically works like this:

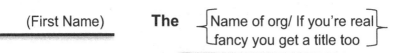

(First Name)   **The**   Name of org/ If you're real fancy you get a title too

I thought that was the most preposterous thing I'd ever heard of until it happened to me. When I got my first title in an organization someone called me "Chris the Treasurer". I let them make it because there were two Chris' in the group. Then, after I pledged it happened again! I was in the quad and overheard someone say, "that's Chris... the Alpha".

WILL MY ORG

MAKE ME BETTER

or

WILL I

MAKE MY ORG BETTER?

YES

I was hotter than fish grease! It would have been different if the people saying it didn't know me before I pledged but these were cats I hooped with and hung out with on a regular basis. It bothered me because I felt like my affiliations were changing who I was. In reality, it was changing how others viewed me. It will happen to you as well. When you accept a formal leadership role folks tend to look at you differently. To borrow from Peter Parker "with great ability comes great responsibility.' In the Peace Corp it's called the fishbowl effect. The Fishbowl Effect is a feeling or reality where every move or decision is observed and scrutinized and used to judge the entire org/group. And if you're not careful, it can cause undue stress to you and make your leadership experiences pretty miserable.

If you allow yourself to get caught up in the hype you may begin to allow others to set the standard for you. Don't let your fraternity/sorority, team, or any organization distort who you are or force you into acting a certain way. You don't have to live up to, or down to, the stereotypes that surround your org/group. My time as a student leader definitely helped to shape my worldview and perspective, but I never believed that it made me. You were selected to lead or join a group because of who you are right now, today. Even if a group likes you for your potential, the ability is still there right now. Your org should never change you. In the frat we always asked, "Would the letters make the man or will the man make the letters?" We were missing one word in that question...better. Ask yourself, "Will my org make me better or will I make my org better?" The answer should be both.

- **How do you or will you make your org better?**

- **How does your org make you better?**

Day 12
Be a Dump Truck?

You may have heard the saying, "a chain is only as strong as its weakest link". Well duh, but no one ever tells you how to fix the darn chain. Until now. If there is a weak link in your chain, you have to be a dump truck! Yeah, a dump truck. Before I explain that, let's have a moment of clarity. Not everyone in an organization or group is there to "be a leader". Sometimes folks join because they're bored, trying to holler at a cute member, or maybe it's mandated by a judge or something. Knowing that everyone is not in the org for altruistic reasons lets us understand that the motives of others are out of our control. However, what we can control is how we operate and how we treat people. You can't make folks do anything, but you can do your part to equip them to work if/when they are ready. Part of moving yourself and your org to a #LEADERSHIPISAVERB mentality is about strengthening the people around you so that as a collective, the org can be dope.

Now, back to the dump truck and fixing the weak link in the chain. Sadly, I see so many talented leaders burnout and get frustrated because of the superhero syndrome. The superhero syndrome is when a student tries to do everything in or for an org. They try to put the group on their back and will an organization to the finish line. Ain't happening boss. Leaders that don't trust their people enough to delegate aren't very efficient.

Leaders don't trust folks for various reasons but it's mostly because they won't take the responsibility of growing members. If several people in your group understand how to run the day to day operations, that frees you up to do the things that only you can do. The best way to have multiple people capable of running an org is to be a dump truck. A dump truck is designed to collect materials, transport them to a certain place, and then DUMP THE MATERIAL! A dump truck has two purposes, get filled up and dump, that's it.

If a dump truck was always empty, it would have nothing to dump and if it was filled and never dumped, how could it be filled again. A dump truck is only doing half of its job if it collects material without ever transporting it and letting it go. Why am I taking you on this circular slippery slope? To drive home the point that when something has a specific purpose, doing anything outside of that purpose hinders it from being what is was created to be. To become a more powerful, effective, and balanced leader you can't be afraid to let go of information and responsibilities. Always remember, if a dump truck is doing its job right, a dump truck is never empty for very long."

One of the biggest obstacles in leadership is the ~~filling~~ feeling of being overloaded. Because you are the leader everything falls on your shoulders. The organization rises and falls with your ability to rally the troops, guide them into battle, and lead them out successfully. But that is a lot to take on by yourself and eventually you become overloaded, overwhelmed, and then your role as leader is over.

- WHEN YOU TEACH SOMETHING -
YOU GAIN A DEEPER UNDERSTANDING...
IT BECOMES A PART OF WHO YOU ARE

Why do we as leaders feel the need to do everything ourselves? Is it because of pride or fear? I'm willing to put my money on both. We are scared to let someone else have control over something that has our name attached to it, because we are scared of their ability to do it like we do it. I was terrified to let the freshman Social Chair pub for one of our biggest events of the year, but he knocked it out the park like Ken Griffey, Jr.!! When I congratulated him on the most successful event in the program's history I asked him how he did it. His answer set me free. He mentioned a conversation we had over lunch where I told him about when I did the event and the struggles and success' I encountered. He called it a brain dump! By hearing my experience he was able to skip over a few miscues that plagued our group in the past. He then told me that he knew he was ready for the event because of the confidence he got from running meetings during the previous semester. We gave him the information/tools and the opportunities to practice using those tools, when it was time to shine he'd already been grinding!

The dump truck concept helps you too. To be effective you have to refresh your perspective on information and knowledge. This refreshed perspective should reflect the idea that your brain can only retain so much information before it needs to be dumped, the more you dump the more you can put back in. Just because you dump, you don't lose the info, it just becomes stored in a different section. When you teach something to someone, you get a deeper understanding of the subject matter and now it becomes a part of who you are instead of just something you know.

No matter how intelligent we are, there is only a finite amount of information our brains can process and retain. Don't be constipated, information is a gift that should be shared freely and readily to your organization so that everyone is on the same page and has the same basic abilities. Sharing of information allows for a more versatile and flexible team.

Now that you have shared and taught everything you know and are confident that your people know what's up, you can now move on to different and more challenging tasks and repeat the cycle all over again. This is only possible because you don't have to do everything by yourself. Being a dump truck is more of a cultural concept for how information should be shared within your org. And don't forget that what you do in one org might translate to another org so dump away!

- **What information do you need to share with your team to insure everyone is on the same page?**

- **How can you create intentional moments/ opportunities into the structure or culture of your org for members to get a chance to grow and develop their leadership skills?**

- **How do you intentionally transfer information from one group of leaders to the next?**

Day 13
Ice Cream and Dreams

After speaking at a conference at the University of Missouri, I was talking to a group of students about the workshop. Somehow we got on the topic of what role a young lady in the group played in her organization and her aspirations for the next year. As the young lady began telling us how she didn't want to hold an office, chair an event, or be at any events that weren't mandatory, it didn't take long to figure out she was in the organization because the members got a free trip to this national conference. After clowning her motives for joining, I asked her a simple question, "What is your favorite ice cream?"

The young lady responded as if I asked did she want a million dollars! She hurriedly squealed out "COOKIES & CREAM!" And not just any cookies and cream either, it had to be the kind made in a small town right outside of Houston (bonus points if you know the name of the place). Without any further prodding this now extremely excited young lady began to passionately describe not only the taste of the ice cream but how good she felt while eating it!

After her 5 minute keynote, I asked her another simple question, "What's your favorite thing about your organization?" And as quickly as Thor lent her his hammer, he took it away and her thunder along with it. Knocked the cool completely out of her step.

Under an embarrassed smirk she answered, "I don't know!?" Immediately, I asked "What's your favorite thing about yourself?" As she stood there biting her lip and staring at the floor, she lifted her head and formed her mouth to answer. When nothing came out, tears began to flow from her eyes. It's amazing how much we know about the nuances of our favorite things/people compared to how much we know about ourselves.

Student leadership can help you understand yourself. Now student leadership won't magically show you your life's purpose, but it can help you discover your passions. You find out the what, how, and why you are motivated and with that knowledge you can better set your expectations on how/why we interact with others. Student leadership should be more than just a resume builder or notch on your belt. We need to redefine how we look at student leadership and begin to view it as an avenue of self-discovery and learning. The soft skills you acquire in leadership roles can help you maximize the hard skills you learn in your course work.

Think about how much more you will accomplish when you take the time to find out where your passions lie. Because you understand how you are motivated you will take on roles that cater to your strengths, tackle your areas of improvement, and eliminate time-stealing tasks, roles, and people from your life. Understanding the potential impact of student leadership on your professional development changes your perspective on those meetings and projects.

STUDENT

LEADERSHIP
SHOULD
— BE MORE —
THAN JUST
a resume builder
OR NOTCH ON
YOUR BELT.

You don't need a formal role or title to be a leader, though it's important to take on those responsibilities when you're ready. What you need is the perspective that every student on your campus is a leader with a purpose and privilege to impact their peers and their communities.

Stop imaging the greatness that can ensue from unleashing your passion and start living in it!!

- **How can you provide leadership to an org without holding a formal title or position?**

- **What is your favorite thing about your org and why? What is your favorite thing about yourself and why?**

Day 14
Paint a Vivid Picture, Design your masterpiece

If we are defined by what we do and what we do is shaped by our goals, the process of goal-setting is vital to our success as student leaders. Often we set goals and don't know what they look like. Before you huff and puff about the goal setting acronym you think is on the way, save it!! I am going to propose a different way to think about goal setting. I want to redefine your student leadership experience and give you a tool to make you a more powerful, effective and balanced student leader. I propose that we take the time to visualize our goals. I mean really see them. I'm talking crystal clear, hanging in a museum, priceless work of art see them. Imagine the hard work, the right work, the setbacks, and the achievements.

So often goals are simply notches on our belt, or necessary evils for us to live a certain lifestyle. Aside from our end line focus, goals are simply items on a to-do list. Normally, when we set goals, we concentrate on the quantitative aspect (one more thing checked off the to-do list) of reaching new heights. This sets up the structure or bones of our dreams and aspirations. It provides a decent outline, but when things begin to fall apart and "it" finally hits the fan, you need more than an outline or skeleton! The visualizing I'm suggesting we do is how you put the meat on the bones! Something you can sink your teeth into when you are forced to regroup.

STOP VIEWING

YOUR GOALS AS TASK ON

≡ A TO-DO LIST ≡

AND START SEEING THEM

FOR WHAT THEY ARE,

BUILDING

BLOCKS ON YOUR

PATH TO PERSONAL

GREATNESS

The next time you set a goal for yourself, I want you to know what it looks like. I want you to be able to close your eyes and see it, take a deep breath and smell it, lick your lips and taste it!! The process works by engaging both your imagination and your quantitative thought process. Normally, these two thought processes occur separately. By combining these two opposite ways of thinking, we are able to balance them both while formulating a more complete idea.

Think about it. When you are planning an event, you have a different thought process for coming up with the budget than coming up with ideas for a social activity. And sometimes, that budget planning thought process will kill a couple of big ideas you have. That's because you have two opposing thought processes going on and we have always been taught that prudence wins out. However, through the process of visualizing your goals, you can combine both processes and achieve bigger and better. Instead of letting your budget kill your big ideas, let your big ideas fill your coffers and grow your budget. Stop viewing your goals as task on a to-do list and start seeing them for what they are, building blocks on your path to personal greatness.

Side note: *When visualizing your goals beware of the "tiara and crowns" trap! It's important that we paint an accurate picture of our success. Think about everything that comes with your goal, both positive and negative. Be realistic about the effort and maintenance that your goals will require. Don't let the smooth taste fool you; reaching our personal greatness is a stubbornly difficult process. Paint that part of the picture too!*

4 Steps to Powerful, Effective and Balanced Goal-Setting:

1. Write down your goals in sequential list form.

2. Take each goal and write a brief 3-5 sentence paragraph about how you will achieve the goal. Include things that may be an obstacle to meeting the goal.

3. Develop at least two (2) solutions, no matter how off the wall they may seem, as long as they're feasible...list them! This is the visualization/defining process.

4. Work right, work smart, & work hard.

Trust is Easier to Keep Than to Rebuild

Trust is essential in productive relationships & develops bonds that run deeper than oceans. However, as strong a bond as trust can build; losing it creates chasms as magnificent as the Grand Canyon. That was a rather verbose way to say trust is important and losing it is catastrophic. Trust is like credit, it's easier to keep than to rebuild. It takes years of consistency and discipline to build excellent credit. You have to make on-time payments, use 35% or less of your available credit, and resist the urge to get that "free" t-shirt for filling out a credit application! But doing so typically results in a 790 credit score.

A credit score of 790 leads to a bigger pool than Kanye and the faith from financial institutions that you will be a good financial steward. However, you can ruin your credit in 6 weeks. Run up too big a tab at the bar and max out your credit card, pay a few bills late or not at all and watch what happens to that 790!! You mess around and get turned down for credit at Conn's! This may not seem fair, but its reality. If you ever think its ok to renege on the financial commitments you have made you may do it again. Sure there are situations that call for exceptions to be made, but we are what we repeatedly do. Consider trust as an emotional capital similar to credit. We all start out with a little trust, but it takes consistency and discipline to solidify that trust.

CONSIDER TRUST AS AN EMOTIONAL CAPITAL

SIMILAR TO CREDIT.

WE ALL START OUT WITH A LITTLE TRUST
BUT IT TAKES
CONSISTENCY AND DISCIPLINE
TO SOLIDIFY THAT TRUST

Things are rarely the same once trust is lost, so do your best to keep it. Losing trust means losing credibility, authority, and integrity. Surprisingly, keeping trust is pretty easy. You don't have to be perfect just honest. As a leader people have to believe you have their best interest in mind. They have to know that you live Day 6. However, we don't live in a perfect world. Life happens and sometimes, whether it be pride, shame, or greed, we lose trust. How you come back from moments like this are as important if not more important than how you respond to success.

One of my first jobs out of college was at Enterprise Rent-A-Car. It was hardcore sales with long hours, washing cars in a shirt and tie, and competitive as all get out. But that job taught me a lot, one of the best things I learned was to Under Promise and Over Deliver. This is crucial because the flip side means to Over Promise and Under Deliver, for which there is nothing worse. It's cool to book a customer for a midsize car and "upgrade" them to a full-size (even though that was all we had on the lot) but Lord help us if a customer booked a full-size car and all we had was a Fiat. The amount of work it took to satisfy a client to whom we Under Delivered was a daunting exercise in futility. As we grow and develop as leaders, remember to not Over Promise. Folks will never forget you put them in a Fiat. Similarly, this is good place to point out that no one really expects perfection. So, as leader, you shouldn't demand or expect perfection either, unless you want that to be the criteria for which you are judged. Push for excellence, but always leave room for grace.

Leaders put their organization in position to develop trust in each other, it builds their integrity and begins to establish an environment that Promotes and Demands Self-Development. Taking the time to develop trusting relationships allows people know how much you care and "[People] don't care how much you know, until they know how much you care." At least that's what Teddy Roosevelt said.

Genuine relationships are the cornerstone of successful organizations because they form a connection that goes beyond an organizational level. It forms bonds that make everyone feel responsible for their actions for not only the sake of the organization but for the sake of the people in the organization. Genuine relationships based on trust and integrity personifies or brings life to your organization.

- **How can you build trust in your org? How are you intentionally creating moments for members to gain trust and confidence in each other and themselves?**

- **How can you build relationships with the folks in your org?**

Day 16
Don't Be Afraid to Fail:
It Happens to the Greatest of Us!

I was born and raised on the South Side of Chicago, IL and never heard of gumbo until I moved to Texas. One year my mom decides to have a gumbo cook-off for Christmas and I think to myself, "Self, it's just a bunch of meat in some gravy, how hard can it be?" After ten tries at making my own roux (and failing) and ruining four bottles of store-bought roux, I conceded… making gumbo was more than just putting meat in gravy. I had to call in the pros for reinforcement, so I called one of my college friends. Her people were from the birthplace of gumbo, Louisiana, and her Aunt walked me through the process step by step. I had failed miserably, but it forced me to regroup, refocus, and rebuild. With her help I blew everyone away with my "secret" gumbo recipe.

The key to my success was my failure. You read that right, the thing that helped me be successful in my pursuit of authentic gumbo was my multiple failures, or more so how I handled the failure. No one sets out to lose or fail, but it happens. Now, I know someone out there is asking themselves, "What in the world is Chris talking about?!" Failure, *WHEN PUT IN ITS PROPER PLACE*, helps to make you a more powerful, effective and balanced student leader. Overcoming failure helps build the perseverance needed to climb the stepping-stones to success.

REGROUP

REFOCUS

REBUILD

#LEADERSHIPISAVERB

Failure forces you to take time to regroup, refocus, and rebuild; a process often ignored due to the stinging after-effects of failure.

Most of us want to pretend the failure never happened. Face it, failure sucks and it can be embarrassing. All of the emotions connected with failure make it a difficult topic to discuss and an even more difficult outcome to handle. Instead of rushing past our failures, we should take advantage of the opportunities they provide us. It provides a chance to be more powerful by giving you a chance to regroup, to be more effective by showing you where you need refocus, and more balanced by teaching you how to rebuild.

Regrouping allows you to get your bearings and be sure you are still headed in the right direction. Refocusing allows you enhance your vision and outlook on the situation, forcing you to pay attention to the details. And rebuilding puts you back on track to your intended destination. When you employ these three steps, you will learn from your failures so you don't make the same mistake twice. Turing failure into power is a process and that process is hard.. so what.

Failure also provides an opportunity for some of the best teaching moments in the world. Until I became a parent I never understood why my mom would always try to talk to me after I lost a game or didn't make the team. I would be mad at the world and she would force me to talk about the game. "Did you do your best? Practice makes permanent, how did you practice this week? Did you study the game plan? Where they better than you?" Momma I love you but this was so annoying, and so effective. When the wound was fresh it was easier to diagnose.

Failure makes more open to instruction than success. Kayne is the perfect example. He told us we wouldn't be able to tell him "nothin" when he got his money right, so I'm not sure why folks are surprised by his actions.

It wasn't until, as president of the most successful organization on my campus, I had a horrible event, that I realized failure brings about a different level of self-awareness and consciousness. It brings you to a place where you are faced to deal with your limitations. When things are going according to plan, your organization talks about how THEY run the yard and it's easy to get comfortable in your success. When things go awry, your organization is questioning whether YOU got complacent and if you ever really ran anything! It is simply a teaching moment. Failure is a time for evaluation and learning. In the Bible, it was in moments of failure that Christ was able to teach the 12 disciples more than they learned from witnessing miracles. Another reason failure is a not so obvious marker for success is because you have to have the perseverance to keep putting failure in its proper place. There is a funny thing about failure, if you remember when I first introduce the word, I said, "when put in its proper place" it's a good thing. It's easy to stumble once and keep moving but to repeat and endure the process for as long as it takes, is a testament to your passion and dedication.

When you don't put failure in its proper place, it turns to fear, which has a crippling effect on an organization. Fear will blind the vision, cripple the will of the willing, poison the unity of the group, and destroy any chances for success. Remember when you fail, it is of the utmost importance that you put that crook in its place. Don't let failure steal your joy, let it be the fuel that propels you to your next action!

So the next time you bomb a test or your event doesn't go exactly as planned, remember:

1.   Failure forces you to **Regroup, Refocus, and Rebuild.**
2.   **Failure provides** some of the best **teaching moments** possible.
3.   **Failure is a GOOD THING** when PUT **IN its PROPER PLACE**!!

Day 17
Get a Mentor
Be a Mentor

I was always a pretty good student, but I sucked in math. Somehow I made it to the 5th grade counting my multiplication on my fingers. That made for a really slow process when it came time to take a test. During a math quiz, my teacher noticed that I was counting on my fingers and called me out on it. After trying to deny it, I found myself in unfamiliar territory, facing academic failure. But our school had a special weapon, his name was Mr. Black. I am not sure what Mr. Black did but he worked with all types of students. I was embarrassed at first because he typically worked with students with behavior problems or mental disabilities. When my teacher told me I was going to be working with Mr. Black I was worried about what folks would think about Chris the smart kid needing to be in Mr. Black's class. Mr. Black changed all that, he came and got me out of my class 3 times a week and tutored me.

I quickly realized he was the coolest cat in the building. But he had rules, if you were in his "crew" you had to have great behavior and be a leader in the class. That was the easy part. However, in our tutoring sessions, let's just say I wasn't too fond of his rules there; he was strict, never let me count on my fingers, timed me on quizzes and held me accountable if I made anything less than a 100 on a quiz or test in class. But Mr. Black was the truth: in a community where there were very few positive black male examples, Mr. Black accepted and relished that responsibility. He taught me how to shake hands (though he mostly just crushed my knuckles when he shook mine) and look a man in the eye when I talked to him. With all he taught me, the thing that stands out the most is when I taught him how to do the kid-n-play and the butterfly! He was so excited (at least he let me think so)!! I didn't teach him anything that changed his life or made him a better man, but teaching him anything was huge for me, I thought he knew everything! As a mentor Mr. Black helped me learn more than just my multiplication tables, he helped me understand that even a mentor can be a mentee.

Some of the best parts of my student leadership experience were my mentoring and mentee relationships. I enjoyed the intentional transfer of information and energy that a mentoring relationship required. Mentorship is so important to leadership because it mitigates the challenges of transition and the changing of the guard. When there is an intentional transfer of information and energy, the next group of leaders don't have to reinvent the wheel and start from scratch. Mentorship is one of the best ways to help your organization stay relevant and motivated. When you and your team work hard to build a great culture in your org and start to live your mission and vision it's awesome! But what happens when you all move on or graduate? What happens to the culture and the things you all have built and created? Without mentorship, those things are in danger of being forgotten and left behind. Without mentorship, you leave the future of the org to chance.

THE INTENTIONAL
TRANFER OF INFORMATION
AND ENERGY IS THE
MOST EFFICIENT WAY
TO GET AND
KEEP YOUR ORG
RELEVANT AND MOTIVATED

___

With mentorship, you can continue to build on the work you started or carry the mantle of the folks that came before you. Mentorship is a way to create and solidify your legacy on your campus. Be a mentor get a mentor, make a lasting impression on your campus. The intentional transfer of information and energy is the most efficient way to get and keep your org THERE.

3 WAYS TO INTENTIONALITY TRANSFER INFORMATION AND ENERGY

1.   Create an Executive Book

This is a folder or drive that contains all the pertinent information needed to conduct day to day business for each position on the e-board and other important positions. Whether it's a list of advisors, important contacts, the process for accessing funding for events, or how to secure a meeting room; this and information like it should be readily available to the next group of leaders

Level Up... *if you actually allow the next group of leaders to practice these task before they have a title. That way it's old hat by the time they step into a formal leadership role.*

2.   Shout out the Old Heads:
Develop an Alumni Access Point

Create a way for alumni to remain engaged and active in the organization. Maybe it's a GroupMe chat that keeps them abreast of big events and on goings. Maybe it's a e-newsletter that keeps them informed about the progress of the org. Any communication needs to go both ways, so be prepared for old heads to have comments, take them as they come and use the good, trash the bad.

Level Up... if you develop an alumni partnership that helps folks in your org with their careers. A great way to do that is to have a business mixer during homecoming or as a standalone event. Most alumni want to help and see you succeed, you simply have to give them an avenue to do so.

3. Create a Wish Book

This should be an "I wish I would have known, did, or said this" book. This gives folks a chance to leave behind ideals, words of wisdom, and warnings to the next group. This shouldn't be reserved for formal leaders, anyone that's an active member can contribute.

Level Up... if you make this digital and anonymous. It will take some filtering because anonymity turns some folks into keyboard gangsters, but it also tends to get more honest responses.

Day 18
<u>Speak Up:</u>
<u>A Closed Mouth Don't Get Fed</u>

Old folks have some of the craziest sayings. "I'll be done in two shakes of lambs tail", "you're crazier than a betsy bug", and my favorite "you do (insert negative behavior) faster than a cat can lick its behind!" I swear hanging out with old people is cool if only for the colloquialisms. Another thing old folks like to say is, a closed mouth don't get fed. That's mad wisdom! For one, it's true; 1.You can't eat with your mouth closed & 2. If you don't tell people you're hungry, no one will ever know you're starving. It's similar to the thought that the squeaky wheel gets the oil. Now that I have used almost all the clichés I know, I want to challenge you to speak up.

One of the hardest things about being a leader is developing the ability to be vulnerable and transparent. I used to feel that if I showed vulnerability or let people know about a deficiency in my skill set I would be viewed as a less capable leader or member. I was really struggling as the NPHC President and Chapter President, and I lost focus on the fact that student came before leader. On a road trip with my advisor, TP, I was talking like everything was great but he knew my GPA and things were not great. I'll never forget that trip, mostly because we got a speeding ticket on the road trip home, but also because I opened up about my struggles to TP. After that we had a different type of relationship, he was always supportive but now he knew how to best support my success, even if that meant asking/telling me to step down from my position and get my life together.

Speak Up

what success story

ARE YOU STARVING

WITH YOUR SILENCE?

#LEADERSHIPISAVERB

If you need help developing a particular aspect of your character or leadership style you must:

1. Be open to the change/development
2. Let someone know you need help.

When I spoke with TP, I was considering dropping out of college. I had mastered the art of starvation through silence. It wasn't until I acknowledged I needed help & opened my mouth that I began to excel. I was able to feed off the support of administrators, friends and family. I got my fill of success and fulfillment. And most importantly, I learned how to feed others in my same situation. Real talk *claps hands* most folks in your life want you to succeed. They want to see you be your best and are willing to help you win! You have to swallow your pride and ask for help! You have to surround yourself with people that allow you to be transparent and vulnerable. True growth happens at the corner of transparent and vulnerable. Being transparent allows for you and the folks that support you to know the areas you need help conquering. Powerful leadership is as much about your character and personal development as it anything else. The more you're willing to invest in yourself the better you will be as an individual and a leader. Being vulnerable forces you to acknowledge you're human and that you have limitations. That should force you to operate in your strengths so you can focus on developing what you do well into something you are great at!

An added benefit to speaking up is that as you get help, you are now prepared to help others. There are folks out here struggling because great leaders like you make it look so easy!! They don't see the late nights, the hard work, the folks not showing up to events. By no means do I want you to go around po' mouthin. There's no po' mouthin' in powerful leadership! But watch for the signs. When you have experienced and conquered burn out, organizational apathy, etc. You know what it looks like when others are going through similar issues. And because you will know how your people get down, you will recognize when they're not operating at their highest level. You'll know when to ask questions, when to pull folks aside, and when to step in, like TP did for me, and make the tough calls.

Remember when you speak up, it gives the people around direction and permission to support you in the way you need it most. When you overcome a challenge, your success story is meant to help fuel or feed someone else conquer their challenges.

How can you sharing your story (success/challenges) help others?

If you could give the younger you advice what would that advice be and what age would you want to know it? Now go find some folks that are in similar situations as you were at that age and tell them that advice!

Don't Believe the Hype!

Flava Flav (before reality TV got a hold to him) was in a group called Public Enemy. In one of PE's hit songs, Flava belted, "don't believe the hype!" Unfortunately, some of us didn't listen. Some of us still fall for the Oke-doke and believe the lies about leadership. And not just any lie, but the biggest lie "THEY" ever told about leadership. When I facilitate leadership retreats at different schools, the same question always rears its ugly head and is typically followed by similar if not identical answers. It goes a little something like this:

Student Leader A: What type of person makes the best leader?

Student Leader B: The best leaders are type A personalities, outspoken, public speakers, you know the Zack Morris kid, the popular student. They are just natural born leaders.

Me: DON'T BELIEVE THE HYPE!! I am an introvert and I was pretty good student leader and speak in front of large crowds all the time.

You have to be charismatic, type A, or an extrovert to be a great leader.
These are the BIGGEST LEADERSHIP LIES ever told!! The best leaders understand that #leadershipisaverb and are willing to do the work it takes to be great!

This journey is about redefining student leadership and more importantly it is about results. Take a moment to think about your ideal leader and you might notice that your image is not far from the above student's image of a Type A personality. It's because that's how leadership is portrayed in media, from cartoons and comics to movies and autobiographies. Leadership is normally portrayed as a handsome white male, with muscular features, great speaking ability, and generally loved by all. Even though these characters don't wear t-shirts that say leader, it's obvious they're in charge. They say art imitates life, but sometimes it's the other way around. Because most of society has become comfortable with this image of leadership, we tend to look toward and vote for people that closely line up with this universal ideal of leadership.

It's no different on our campuses and sometimes we get it right – we elect Type A personalities and/or extroverts as leaders and they get the job done. But DON'T BELIEVE THE HYPE!!

There is no one type of person that makes for a better leader, unless you want to call 'accountability' a personality trait. There is no such thing as a natural born leader. We are born with a few abilities and I'm sorry… but leadership is not one of them. Our experiences and conditions shape who we are as people and as leaders.

HE NEXT TIME YOU THINK
'OU ARE TOO QUIET TO LEAD,
OR TOO YOUNG
R ANY OTHER LIMITING THOUGHT....

DON'T BELIEVE THE HYPE!!

"We are the sum of our reactions to life's challenges." (THAT needs to be in somebody's fortune cookie) Just because you are not the most outgoing or outspoken person in a group, doesn't mean you are not best suited to lead. The qualifications for leadership differ from group to group, but there are some traits all great leaders have in common. All great leaders have a handle on what makes them powerful, effective, and balanced.

Your POWER comes from your:

• **Passion** – not the outwardly showing 'let me give you a rah-rah speech' kind either, but the intrinsic motivation that fuels your drive.

• **Vision** – the ability to look at the present with the future in mind. Great leaders are able to forecast where their organization needs to go and just like your favorite meteorologist they make it plain so you can adjust accordingly.

Your EFFECTIVENESS comes from your:

• **Accountability** – most leaders make the most of their ability and the abilities of those around them. They hold themselves responsible for striving towards excellence and make it easy for others to do the same.

Your BALANCE comes from you being:

• **Thick-Skinned** – great leaders welcome criticism, both constructive and destructive, they take it and roll with it. They sift through it and find the things that can help them and their group and move on. It's not easy taking on a leadership role and you will never please everyone. If you take every negative comment about you to heart you'll be in trouble.

The list of attributes for a great leader is a mile long and being outgoing or outspoken certainly makes the list, but they are nowhere near the top. Leadership is not an adjective. It's not something that describes who you are. #LEADERSHIPISAVERB, it describes what you do.

The next time you think you are too quiet to lead, or too young or any other limiting thought......***DON'T BELIEVE THE HYPE!!***

Day 20
Same Menu Different Venue:
Get ya Menu Right

Success principals can be found just about anywhere, even while reading the fine print on the menu of one of my favorite restaurants. I was eating at the Grand Lux Café and read that they were owned and operated by the Cheesecake Factory. In itself this discovery did nothing except let me know that I can get the great food of the Cheesecake Factory at the cheaper price of the Grand Lux Café. However, on a deeper level I was observing an amazing but simple and easily implemented success strategy. The Cheesecake Factory realized that they had a great product on their hand but there was one problem, they were missing a lot of business because of the prices on their menu. But instead of messing with an already good thing, they simply took the same menu and changed the venue. They scaled down the ambiance but kept the essence of the Cheesecake Factory the same. The change in venue allowed for lower prices and access to a broader market.

In a similar vein, the same things that make people successful in their personal lives can be easily translated to their organizations and in turn make the organization more successful. **The key is to prepare a menu or process that is applicable to varied desired outcomes**. To prepare this menu or process, you do not have to reinvent the wheel; just realize there is a consistent inherent value to the steps that lead to success. That inherent value is based on five core competencies, that once mastered will revolutionize the way you lead and conversely the way your organization operates.

Five Core Competencies:
1. **Aim for Systemic, Tangible, Results**
   (within a process that can be duplicated)
2. **Have a Service Focus**
3. **Gear all activity toward building Integrity and Trust**
4. **Promote and Demand Self-Development**
5. **Value Diversity**

Every one or thing that is consistently successful has a process or pattern that creates results that can be duplicated. A Result Driven process is what it is, a process that is driven or guided to lead its participants to a particular result or goal. These are often systemic, tangible results that are easily identified and quantifiable. The most successful and long lasting organizations have processes that Drive Results. The goal is to set their people up for success as best as possible, so they develop their process around the things most important to their organizations. This is why Greek organizations pledge or have an intake process, schools have orientation, jobs have on-boarding, and the armed forces have boot camps. It doesn't matter what type of organization it is; there is an on-boarding process that orients their new members in the history, best practices, and current culture and goals of the organization.

It's like working backwards, sort of. Identify your desired results and build your process from there. Your organizations mission statement gives you your goals... so SHOOT! Evaluate where you are, refocus and shoot again!! When you have a goal it allows you to measure and evaluate your progress. As we discussed in Find the Win – Win, student organizations sometimes focus so much on running the yard that it becomes the only result they strive for, but the organizations that consistently run the yard are the organizations with results that are focused on Service.

Service is a major part of every organization's mission statement and sometimes it's even a part of their constitution or motto. Once again, there are no coincidences on the journey to great student leadership. If you want the masses to identify with you, develop an ideal that serves the masses. This is true on an organizational and personal level. Most of us have heard that Great Leaders are Great Followers, and because it has become so cliché, we have overlooked the genius behind the concept... SERVICE!! Let's break it down in equation form:

Great Leaders = Great Followers = Great Servers
and if we skip the middle man,
Great Leaders = Great Servers.

As a leader you must determine the needs in your organization and figure out how you can best meet those needs, when your Focus on Service is genuine it's infectious. Everyone from the president to the cat that just joined has the proper attitude and buy in and everyone is drinking the Kool aid. This genuine servant attitude creates the perfect atmosphere for building Integrity and Trust amongst the group. Every activity must be geared toward building Integrity and Trust. Put people in a position where they are challenged and have no choice other than to lean on their neighbor.

GREAT LEADERS = GREAT FOLLOWERS

GREAT FOLLOWERS = GREAT SERVERS

SO

GREAT LEADERS = GREAT SERVERS

These relationships expose the way people respond to situations and how to best respond to them. Once you know how your group operates, you are better able to identify strengths and areas of improvement and develop a game plan to take advantage of those aspects. This is where the magic happens, not Disney World but in the leadership retreats, late nights, and countless arguments about who dropped the ball and why. Challenging people to attack their weaknesses and further develop their strengths pushes the aspect of Personal Development.

The power in your process comes from the personal development of the people that take part in it. This development is not natural, as leaders we have to intentionally and strategically put people in place to be challenged and succeed by overcoming that challenge. Sometimes this is called grooming people for leadership. Personal development should go beyond preparing folks for a formal title or role. I learned a lot about myself as a student and as a man during the development I experienced in student leadership roles. The people around me helped to nurture and mature my gifts and talents. The organizations I participated in asked about my life goals and plans and put me in positions to reach those goals. It wasn't always easy, in fact the most exponential growth was produced by challenging and animated conversations. The leaders before me demanded and promoted personal development and that set the expectation for me to do the same. Personal development happens when you push yourself and your organization to Drive for Results that are Focused on Service, while initiating activities that Build Integrity and Trust.

Every competency is essential to building an ideal menu or process, because they are interconnected. If your menu is lacking one it hinders the entire process. But don't worry, if you start from the top, you set yourself up to include the rest. **Stick to the 5 CORE COMPETENCIES** and your MENU WILL SUCCEED IN ANY VENUE.

How can your organization use/implement the 5 Core Competencies of a Results Driven Process?

Day 21
Lead Like you
Sing in the Shower

That moment when you're in the shower and your favorite song is stuck in your head. There's nothing like it! You will hit high notes like Mariah Carey, sing in perfect bass like that one guy from Boyz II Men, and create your own ad libs like you have been singing since you were a one-year-old! Or what about when you and a close friend are in the car and your jam comes on? You sing that song like you are performing at the Grammy's, oblivious to the folks staring at you at the red light.

Thing is... most folks can't sing... not even a little bit. But it's something about the shower and the car that gives us the confidence to out sing a Grammy award winning artist. What is it about those places that gives us that confidence? I know it's not that we're naked! Is it the curtain? Can't be or cats would be walking around with curtains and capes! Maybe, it's the airbag in our car or the seat belt that makes us feel safe. Or maybe, it's the comfort of not having anyone to impress but yourself.

Not having the pressure or expectation of someone laughing at your high note clowning you for your screeching rendition of "My Girl" gives you a special confidence. What if you could have that same type of confidence in your leadership abilities?

WHAT COULD YOU ACCOMPLISH ON YOUR CAMPUS AND IN YOUR COMMUNITY IF YOU HAD THE CONFIDENCE YOU WOULDN'T FAIL?

What could you accomplish on your campus and in your community if you had the unfailing confidence? I know it would make you a more powerful leader. Not like dictator powerful, but visionary, influential powerful.

Here are 3 ways to develop shower, car sing along confidence and become a powerful leader:

1. Sell Out!!

The most important factor of your shower confidence is that you're not worried about messing up! You aren't going for perfect pitch, you're just belting out your favorite tune! It's about the feeling and emotion behind it. You are singing the song because you like it not because you're trying to demonstrate your ability to replicate complex tonal notes. You should lead the same way; unafraid to fail and doing it from your heart because you really enjoy what you're doing. Of course you want to get it right, but the passion that drives you to get involved and lead should outweigh your fear of failure.

2. Make it Your Own

My mom and I used to sing a song in the car together all the time. We would really get into it, so much so that we'd be out of breath when the song was over. One day I was listening to the song at home and actually listened to the song instead of singing it and made a shocking discovery... we were butchering the words to a wonderful Stevie Wonder song.

The next time the song came on in the car my mom and I started singing and I tried to use the right words, it just didn't feel right. We had made that song ours, just like you should do with your leadership. Own it! Lead in your own way. There is no set way to lead, no standard leadership method so you can adjust as you go and shape the way you lead to suit your abilities and the needs of your group. Don't be so caught up in leading like your predecessor that you forget to be you! Your group had confidence that you could do the job, you should believe that too.

3.   Keep Pushing!

Confidence comes from comfort and comfort is developed by consistency. I don't know about you but the first time I start to sing a song I'm a little shaky about it. Oh but once I get comfortable it's a wrap!   That's when I really start to get down! You know you're really comfortable with the song when you know all the pauses, breaks, and ad libs.   My boys and I used to rap Biggie Smalls song Juicy word for word without missing a beat. We had all the pauses and everything. Our favorite part was when he said, "baby baby ugh." We never missed it.

We also sang it every day at least 5 times a day often on repeat. (Don't judge me.) It was the consistency that made us comfortable and that comfort lead to confidence. The more you lead and get involved the more comfortable you will become. Stay consistent and keep pushing to develop a comfort level with the responsibilities of your position. You can do this by working on committees and events before you step into a formal leadership role. Whatever you do, keep pushing because consistency is key to developing your confidence.

When you take the time and put in the effort to work on your leadership skills you will become a more powerful student leader. It's a process so breathe easy if you aren't ready overnight. But these three things will give you "Shower Car Sing Along Confidence" and that will make you a more powerful leader.

The Wrap Up

We live in a society that constantly compares. There are even national rankings for 6yr olds on football teams; that's crazy. However, especially as leaders, it's easy to get caught up in the craze of that competition. But if you must compare, do it right! Don't compare your chapter one with someone else's chapter 100. Leadership is a lifelong process and at different points in your life you will have various responsibilities and opportunities. As long you continue to build and develop, the rest will take care of itself. If you quit after a failure, that failure becomes your legacy. It leaves a stain that blots out all of your good works. But WHEN WE BUILD FROM FAILURE, IT BECOMES a lesson in humility, pushing you into a #LEADERSHIPISAVERB lifestyle. The concepts discussed in this book are practical and applicable things you can implement in your life and/or organization today! Don't go to your next meeting and kick in the door waiving the 44 like Notorious B.I.G., remember this is a process. A journey. Introduce each concept separately and FIRE. AIM. READY. You will get it and your org will be better for it. Never marginalize your efforts or responsibilities; it makes room for others to do so as well. So the next time you think your role is insignificant or of little importance, remember that your pride and work ethic are always significant and important!! Your attitude can influence an entire organization just by you being you. Keep pushing.

Sometimes, especially when we experience success, we get "too big for our britches"; forgetting who we are and where our energy should be focused. That's when a mirror comes in handy! If you ever forget, look in the mirror for a reminder. If you begin to lose touch with those less fortunate or those with less authority, look in the mirror for a moment of SANKOFA (reflecting on your past while contemplating your future). If you ever feel like your image is more important than your reality, hold that mirror up to redirect all the energy you've been focusing outward to spark your passion for your original purpose. A mirror is a pretty handy tool. This will help prevent a ton of avoidable drama.

However, we have all been hurt, seen the drama or dished out the drama and hurt. Some of us reading this are still hurting. Popular advice after an emotional hurt is to "move on" but if we move on without healing, we leave ourselves open for a repeat performance. Examine the things that have you hurting and struggling to move on and attempt to gain understanding about what REALLY happened (not just your version). If you need help (friendly or professional) seek that and get an understanding of what is hurting you, then you can move on to why and move away from the pain. Remember that SPEAK OUT thing we talked about?

During talks, I say, "here are the keys to a brand new Escalade, black on black, fully loaded with all the bells and whistles on 24's...PAID FO' (taxes & all –take that Harpo)!" Then I wait, it's amazing how long it takes for someone to take the keys. This student leadership thing is the same way, fully paid for with all the bells & whistles, waiting on us to take the keys and drive. What are you waiting for? What experiences on your campus are you ignoring that could benefit your career or academic goals? What are leaving on the table because you won't jump at the opportunities? With the tools and confidence you have after this 21 Day Challenge, you can truly say #LEADERSHIPISAVERB.

A Little More Motivation

"Coming together is a beginning. Keeping together is Progress. Working together is Success. Excelling together is GREATNESS!" - Henry Ford (adapted by Chris Collins)

At a certain point, it's not about what you deserve it's about what you earn! Speaking things into existence only works when you act on your words! Speak it. Believe it. Work it. Achieve it.

Always remember, your performance is a product of your process

10 minutes of face to face communication is worth more than a week of emailing back and forth.

#Leadershipisaverb which means it requires action, you have to get out and do something, meet people, shake hands and kiss babies!!

Revolutionary thoughts are rarely radical; simply, they are the realization of the voice and will of the people. What makes them revolutionary is that they are heard and adhered to by the establishment. How will you be the next revolutionary force of our time?

About The Author

Chris is a speaker, author, and consultant with a message that is inspiring students across the country. His unique blend of humor, knowledge, and energy provide high impact moments with results that last long after the presentation. As a former student leader and current college speaker, Chris gets it! As a hip hop head, foodie, and blogger, Chris' take on student leadership is one of the most interesting in the country. His passion for encouraging, empowering, and educating young people forces him to stay on his grind and develop practical, relevant, results-oriented programs. Chris has delivered talks to all types of crowds, including two of the largest high school districts in the country, national conferences, Fortune 500 companies, and colleges and universities of every shape, size, and hue. He doesn't always give speeches but when he does they're your favorite speeches favorite speech!

Book Chris for your next event. Whether it's a leadership conference, keynote, workshop, retreats, or staff development, Chris has a message that will rock your crowd and leave you looking like an all-star.

My Back

The following folks have always had my back and this book will be no different (in no particular order)

My Family, All of yall. Blood is thicker than mud.

Tyrone Brownlee and 121Creative – Designed my cover, logo, business cards, flyers, etc. but more than that, you believed in the vision and invested in me, I hope one day to give you a return on that investment.

Pastor O, Lady O, Johnny Ogletree, III and the First Met Family

Pastor Blake Wilson, James O'Berry, Arthur Walker

Mike D,

Pastor Erick W. Hoskin, Sr. and The WOGCF Family, you helped me get back.

Brandon J. Edwards – you define REAL FRIENDSHIP

Geralda Baugh and We Made it Studios - King of Craft

Keylan Morgan for always keeping me working

Mike Bertrand for leading me through a wall

Dr. Alvin Curette, Jr., Daniel Cunningham,

Jarvis and Erica N. Clark and the whole Clark Family

My Texas State University Family – There are too many to name, so just know I love all of you in Res Life, MSC, BMU, NAACP, Admissions, etc. all of y'all

Mu Nu Chapter of Alpha Phi Alpha (Cliff, Avin, & Rashod for making it worth it if I worked it)

If I forgot someone, don't blame it on my mind or my heart, blame it on my wallet! Publishing a book is expensive!

Made in USA - Kendallville, IN
42275_9781096574705
03.25.2022 1422